Outwalking the Shadow

Outwalking the Shadow

Debra Kaufman

Copyright © 2023 by Debra Kaufman

All rights reserved. This book or parts thereof may not be reproduced in any form, stored in any retrieval system, or transmitted in any form by any means—electronic, mechanical, photocopy, recording, or otherwise—without prior written permission of the publisher, except as provided by United States of America copyright law. For permission requests, write to the publisher, at "Attention: Permissions Coordinator," at the address below.

Redhawk Publications
The Catawba Valley Community College Press
2550 US Hwy 70 SE
Hickory NC 28602

ISBN: 978-1-959346-30-2

Library of Congress Number: 2023949864

Printed in the United States of America

redhawkpublications.com

Layout and Cover by Ashlyn Blake

Author photograph by Sylvia Freeman

*In memory of my mother,
Kathleen M. Kaufman, 1930–2020*

To confront a person with his shadow is to show him his own light.
> Carl Jung, *Psychology and Religion*

And I will show you something different from either
Your shadow at morning striding behind you
Or your shadow at evening rising to meet you.
> T. S. Eliot, *The Wasteland*

Contents

I.

Walking Westerly, My Shadow Precedes Me	3
Dagguerologue	4
To Be Holy	5
School Picture, Second Grade	6
Forgotten	7
Wild Horses	8
Holy Hell	9
Skinny, Half-Wild	10
Someone called my name on the stairs	11
The Farm, 1938	12
The Farm, 1958	13
Hired Hand	15
The Babysitter	17
Chime	18
After Church	19
Half Wolf	20
You've lived many lifetimes like this:	21
Dear Good Girl	22
I am the ill-kept secret	23
The Assistant	24
Heading West	26

II.

Write, the widow urges	31
The last time my mother	32
Corona Virus as Ballet Dancer	33
Pearl	34
Neighbor	35
Iryna	36
To Be True	37
Crows Above the Cemetery	38
I always see bluebirds	39
Census 2020	40
Some People	42
Boat Cloud	43
It is time to stop waiting	44
A Measure of Happiness	45
Let my heart swing open	46
First Daughter	47
When I call you saintly	48
It Takes a Heart Like Mary's These Days	49
For Days I've Felt Myself Unraveling	50
My Mother's Funeral	51
Dear Cemetery	53

III.

Bearing/Witness	57
Shadows	59
Doing Yoga and Swatting Flies to a Recording by Vladimir Horowitz	60
On the Anniversary of My Mother's Death	62
After Yogi Berra and Robert Frost	63
After centuries of grief, the women in black	64
Women Will Die	65
Eve, Again	66
Sing or Die	68
Ritual	69
Prayer	70
What cannot be said will be wept	71
Memorial Day	72
Today	73
I asked if his compassion	74
Canada Day	75
End of Vacation	76
When You Invite in a Dream	77
A Wish for a New Year	78
Campfire	79
To the wren with the loud song	80
Notes	*82*
Acknowledgments	*83*
About the Author	*85*

I.

Walking Westerly, My Shadow Precedes Me

She does not hear a warning
in the wren's song,
              as I do,
or see the ghost moon as an omen.

She appears
to have a jauntier step,
wilder hair, longer, slimmer limbs.

Perhaps she is the me
I once was—
waitress, dancer, diary keeper.

Nothing bad
has happened yet.
              Soon

she will trail a dangerous
fragrance, be sniffed out,
tracked, pinned down.

Wind trembles the beech leaves.
The wren calls again.

I step toward the past,
she into the future.

Dagguerrologue

> *n. An imaginary conversation with an old photo of yourself.*
> *The Dictionary of Obscure Sorrows*

When Mother made you pose
in your Annie Oakley outfit,
her anxiety—*does it fit right,
do you like it?*—is caught
in your half smile, clasped hands.

What held you back from your desire
to please her, but also to be free
to out-shoot any man at full gallop?
When the camera clicked, did you sense
the difference between the actual you
and the one you imagined?

Each passing year a fine silt drifted
over you, over us: others' expectations
or their lack of imagination.
Be a teacher, nurse or secretary,
marry and raise children—
so many small ways to give yourself away.

I resisted sometimes but in such a quiet,
stubborn way perhaps you did not notice.
Did I disappoint you?
Maybe that innate core of you, of us,
never had enough wildness,
the fierce loneliness it takes to be that woman
riding westward across the prairie,
waving her hat, never growing old.

To Be Holy

At age six when I heard
        a preacher bird call,
He is here! Jesus hears you,
        I imagined myself
in a sheer white gown

        with luna moth wings,
a tiara for a halo,
        carried by the wind
to faraway countries.
        The poor souls

would thank me
        for the gifts I brought,
clothes I sewed myself,
        homemade lemonade,
cupcakes with swirled icing.

How kind I'd be,
        keeping every promise,
my voice lilting,
        I can't stay long,
dear friends. Farewell!

No place forbidden.
        Nothing to harm me.
A cloud for a bed.
        The moon following me
like a good dog.

School Picture, Second Grade

This girl half-smiling as if bursting with a secret
doesn't care that her mother cut her bangs crooked,
loves this hand-me-down dress, the twirl of it.
She is tops in jacks but does not brag.
When she swings on a swing, her feet touch the clouds.
Sometimes she feigns sleep so her father
will carry her off to bed, her prince.

Who could bear to tell her that too soon
her childhood will be trampled by cruel classmates,
the death of her grandfather, her own fears and shyness?
Better to whisper, *Be valiant, little one,*
keep your heart open and soft.

Forgotten

Who sent my sister and me away,
into the wind swirling our skirts, and why
was it our uncle who found us uptown

and told us our grandfather had died
from a stroke, whatever that meant,
and drove us back in his humming car

to our grandmother's house, where
we lived then, with its dark hush,
cigarette smoke, cousins crowding the kitchen,

and why was our mother busy brewing coffee,
why didn't our father take us aside
to explain how his father could be truly

forever dead when just last week
he'd spoon-fed him ice cream?
Everyone all muddled together,

no one minded how much cake we ate,
no one warned us what would happen next.

Wild Horses

As the new girl, you must learn
the rules of recess lightning-quick.
The boys are cowboys,
the girls wild horses.
If they catch you,
they get to corral you.
How fast can you flee,
your bare legs lean,
wind in your hair,
jacket wide open?
You reach the creek edge,
breathless, untouched,
watch as boys lead girls
by the wrists
to the school's cool shadow.
The girls whinny,
paw the ground, nibble
pretend-apples from the boys'
grimy hands.
You see you are neither
the tamer nor the tamed.
You toss your mane.
Until now, you never knew
you could outrun everyone.

Holy Hell

I didn't know what or where it was,
only that it was bad and Jay said
we'd catch it if his dad found out
he'd swiped the matches.
Dark lurked in the playground shrubs.
The swings creaked in the wind.
It's cold as hell, he swore again,
his chapped hands scurrying
like small wild animals.
He had me gather leaves and twigs.
I was good at doing what I was told.
I held my breath. The match flared
and he touched it to the nest we'd made.
Run! and we did, the secret burning
in our combustible, thrilling little hearts.

Skinny, Half-Wild

My sister and I shinnied up trees,
hung upside down, reveled in the glory
of being high and unseen,
the breeze and buzz of it,
the shush and shirr, the long jump down.

We played Red Light Green Light
in the neighbors' wide yards,
biked to the playground to wax-paper the slide,
clamber over the rusty cannon,
spin ourselves dizzy on the merry-go-round.

We always shrank from the boy with strange eyes
who came when the park lay in shadow.
In bed, safe and clean in our nighties,
we made up tales about him, sure if one of us
was ever alone he would drag us

into the scraggle across the railroad tracks.
And do what, we did not know
but shivered at the wondering.
I wrote his name in my pink diary,
kept the key safe under my pillow.

Someone called my name on the stairs

kindly, as if to tell me supper was ready.
It was so quiet that day—
my brother napping, my sister away—

I floated down the narrow stairwell.
We lived with our grandmother
and the ghost upstairs who hovered whenever

our mother read us fairy tales.
Once upon a time meant the story happened
long ago somewhere far far away.

The world was fluid then,
only a veil separating here from there,
fireflies and fairies equally alive.

When I got to the kitchen I asked
my mother why she'd called me.
She said she hadn't.

It must have been Jesus, I said.
Before I could wonder
what He might have wanted,

she laughed. The air crackled,
a mirror cracked,
and the magic flew off in a puff of dust.

The Farm, 1938

The mother patches overalls
by oil-lamp light. Electricity
is still new here: *Don't waste it*,
she tells the daughter who hides
in the stairwell to read.
The older girl curls her hair with rags.
The sons play dominoes—
no cards allowed, no radio either,
though the father sings hymns
for the cows at the evening milking.
A barn owl sails down from the hay mow,
the end of another dry scorching day,
clouds gone gray, shredded cotton.
Everything's patchwork.
Yesterday a hobo trudged down
the dirt road looking for work or a handout.
A cousin writes from Germany
they're building up the infantry.
Bad enough, the father thinks,
they had to fight each other
in the war that did not end war.
Leave us alone, he prays, meaning
his family, whose dreams are small,
practical and breakable.

The Farm, 1958

Flies cling to the kitchen screens
while Grandma Naomi stews tomatoes.
The uncles are out, doing chores.

My job is not to get underfoot.
My mother left me here, where
they have no games, no puzzles,
no books except an old Bible.

I love the barn—dark, cool,
fragrant with hay—but Naomi says
it is no place to play. She shoos me

outside: Don't touch the electric fence
or go anywhere near the sows—
they'll devour a girl your size.
Don't wander into the cornfield;

you may never come out. Mind,
there are rats in the corn crib,
the kittens under the porch will scratch.

My legs aren't long enough to make
the swing swing. I count to a hundred
by twos. Grasshoppers whiz by.
When the cows start calling

the uncles come in, caked with mud.
They take off their work boots
and Caterpillar caps and we walk in together.

Supper is ham, green beans, potatoes,
beets, thick milk from a glass jar,
peach pie for dessert.
But first we must wait for Grandpa

to stop praying. On and on he goes.
The window fan whirs. I close my eyes,
let the buzzing carry me far, far away.

Hired Hand

Jake had a hips-first cowboy
way of walking and a gravelly voice
that wasted no words. Nothing
came easy, every dime hard-earned
since age fourteen when he showed up
at the Hardt farm willing to plow,
milk, mend fence, bale hay,
groom the wife's horses.

No one else had hired help—
that's what large families were for.
Julie, my age, reported on his habits:
Jake smoked Chesterfields,
wore a thin denim jacket, no gloves, all winter.
A three-legged Irish setter followed
him on his rounds: *Red*, he'd call,
just the one syllable.

He lived behind the house in a shed
he'd fixed up—tacked over with burlap
so no one could see in.
His truck held no secrets,
though the windshield was flecked
with tobacco bits he'd spit, and
a St. Christopher's medal swung
from the rear-view. He worked
for the family his whole long life.

I don't know what made me think
of him lately—hearing a scratchy song
by Hank Williams, maybe. I called
Julie to see if she had any snapshots.
No, she said, sounding surprised,
Jake always stood just out of range.

The Babysitter

She breezed in, chewing clove gum,
slung her sparkly bag on our new couch,
this teenager I'd never seen before,
Donna, the name of a girl in a song.
She wore white pedal pushers
and a pink angora sweater.
Want to look pretty? Of course I did.
Opening her bag, she brushed blush
on my cheeks, dabbed on some
green eye shadow. *Don't tell your mom.*
She played a stack of 45s she'd brought.
Just like "Down in the Boondocks,"
her boyfriend came from the wrong side of town.
When she was my age
she'd had rheumatic fever, which I heard
as *romantic*, which had damaged her heart,
which is why she cried just thinking about
her mother saying something bad about Sal.
We danced ourselves dizzy, then watched
The Twilight Zone. I fell asleep in my clothes.
At breakfast, pouring my father's coffee,
my mother said, *That girl left glitter
all over my linoleum floor.*

Chime

We were birds then
      at thirteen, a chime
           of wrens chirping,
                  carbonated goddesses
           blowing bubbles,
    spilling secrets,
dancing the latest dances,

we did each others' hair,
      practiced kissing,
           gossiped (a girl's
                  initiation into insight),
           we shook the magic eight ball,
      could not imagine
a path toward our future—

we only knew we didn't want
      our mothers' lives,
           taking dictation,
                cleaning up messes,
           hiding tins of money—

    we were angels falling,
         wingless, trusting
              the wind to lift
        our bodies of light
     far above the silver
water tower,
       to let us down kindly
           somewhere, anywhere
                wild and broad and new.

After Church

When the preacher's son told me
my aura was part halo, part rainbow,
I saw him see me
saintly. God
appeared instantly and everywhere
that summer:
smiling in the pansies,
reflecting us in the farm pond,
beside us on our bikes,
in the barn fragrant with warm cows,
glinting from the hay chaff,
the slatted light.
God touched us as we touched,
electricity in our fingers,
we were shimmery and dewy,
our skin golden, hair sun-bleached.
Angels sang in our voices.
The moon rose in heaven, love,
heaven in the moon.

Half Wolf

Hitching after my shift one bitter night I got in when he offered. The man had a force field around him, cigarette smoke in his clothes, a kind of fierce pulse. He knew where I lived. I knew him by name. I sensed right away he liked me.

Merle Haggard on the radio, six-pack on the floor, a dog in the back seat he claimed was half wolf. He'd found it in the shed, shivering and starving. Could have shot it but fed it instead, named it Cain. He liked having another mongrel around, he said, one scrappy bastard to another.

He drove through the wasted town, its one bar closing, past the high school we'd both hated, down county and gravel roads flat and T-squared. Everything's scarred, he said. 2:00 a.m. and we were both wide awake. I shivered. He turned up the heater.

He stopped at the cemetery. I followed him to his mother's grave. Snow had drifted over the writing, *Jesus called her home.* Orion straddled that deep black sky, the tip of his sword glittering, dogs faithful at his feet. Our breath came without words, small clouds that vanished.

Better get you back, he said, and I wondered what a real home should feel like.

You've lived many lifetimes like this:

holding back, hands folded,
embodying the family code:
do not give yourself away.

No wonder you let the Shadow
lure you into fast cars,
tilt the whiskey flask to your lips:

Girls like you like the sweet burn.
No moon. Scent of cut hay.
Gravel roads that end in trouble.

As long as you succumb
to the trance of *he made me,*
who can blame you?

A voice says, *Remember this:*
No one owns you.
You owe nothing to no one.

Bats dive from the abandoned loft,
arrow-winged, fork-tailed.
Surely it has never been this dark.

Dear Good Girl

All your life you've wrapped your goodness,
a wounded rabbit, in a blanket,
offered it to anyone who seemed in need,
believing the gift would always be replenished.
When you sang, pearls and flowers
spilled from your lips.

Now, betrayed, you see how every
cruel deed has diminished you.
You discover a black bitter spot on your heart.
When you speak your voice croaks,
toads and snakes spew from your mouth.
The bad witch sets a place at your table.

Leave the bundle on a doorstep,
she whispers, come join the outlaws.
You'll find them at their hideout, those
who have given up on kindness so completely
that if anyone should gently touch their shoulders
they'd weep for days, never be the same.

I am the ill-kept secret

a scribbled note tucked into your pocket.
I am smokey scotch,

a clove cigarette smoldering,
a Tiffany ankle bracelet,

the hieroglyph
on the inside of your thigh.

I am the thirteenth fairy at the party,
the shadow in a sheer blouse

and leather slit skirt,
my voice all purr and claws.

I am the perfume you never forget.
I remember everything.

Like the moon I go dark
but never really disappear.

The Assistant

On the job it's head down, hair neat, blouse tucked.
Take good notes, keep the keys and secrets.
Volunteer nothing.

I discovered early there's a quiet way to learn,
just listen to voices like waves lapping.
You don't have to talk.

My father moved us often in our silver
New Moon trailer. Each town
had its own smell. I never minded

not knowing where we'd go next—what mattered
is our family stayed together. I studied
my mother's face to see if what I knew was right.

And the teacher's. I did my sums, clapped
chalk off erasers, ran around at recess
in a kind of delirium. Then we'd leave.

Afterwards, I'd wonder: Should I not
have let the neighbor dab lipstick on me?
Why did I watch Jay strike match after match?

A girl named Jo, who said she was a foster,
wanted me to run away with her. I knew
I wouldn't but didn't tell her so.

Later I learned boys yearned not for words
but for any girl's body. I wanted to choose well
who to kiss, whisper to. So few were worth it.

My heart though. It feels like the jar of seashells
I gathered. They glistened on the shore, but
dry, behind glass, they look ordinary and dull.

Heading West

Raised on fairy tales and country air,
    the sisters expected buffeting winds,
        kept their not-knowing minds open,

expected to somehow prevail. They mapped
    the fine points of their astrology charts
        and set out on a fair day—not chasing

a dream but drifting along one,
    hitchhiking always west, a quiet dare
        buzzing in their souls.

In Kansas, when the money ran out,
    a kindly couple invited them to the farm—
        meals and prayers in exchange

for light chores. *At The Way we share everything.*
    Soon the sisters were filled with goodness
        and light that shone through them

and made their hair shine. They lit campfires,
    did laundry, swept floors, planted beets
        and turnips in the dry, spare earth.

So much to do! Bees hummed, C*ome get our honey.*
    Chickens muttered, *Here's another egg.*
        So much to learn! They combed through

the blessed study guides, chanted with the Reverend,
> *We care as He cares.* They spoke in tongues,
>> sang songs of praise, practiced the nine

manifestations of the holy spirit. *God is here*
> *and everywhere.* One sister stayed a year.
>> The other is still there.

II.

Write, the widow urges

in the dawn-scattered light,
and she comes so rarely,

this wisp of a woman,
that I listen whenever

she whispers. Her hair windswept,

her gown gauzy, she hovers,
alert for an image, a song,

a glimpse, anything that beguiles.
I hold my breath,

half close my eyes, and wait.
The air vibrates,

all my senses lean in,
signal *yes, I'm ready.*

But a crow coughs
and she slips through

the east-facing window,
trailing the scent of rosemary.

The last time my mother

spoke words I heard
I saw her see me in a flash:
You're my daughter!
We walked the hall,
a circumference
around the single rooms.
Round and round.
Each time we passed
the common room
she'd point to the Christmas lights.

On her bed lay a book
of her wedding photos.
I named the names, some small comfort.
I sang "Jacob's Ladder"
and she smiled in that puzzled way.

I meant to rub lotion on her legs—
her skin dry, tissue-paper thin—
but they were calling her
for supper. I kissed her cheek.
She kissed my hand,
did not want to let it go.

I hoped we'd see a few sparrows
out her window, but
dark coming early, I saw only
our ghostly selves reflected there.

Corona Virus as Ballet Dancer

Glittering, unwanted
understudy in the wings,
this is your moment:

the prima ballerina
arches her supple back,
exposing her lovely,
vulnerable throat.
She missteps, falls.

You, dark ingenue,
rush onstage
in your rhinestone tiara,

declare yourself
black swan,
triumphant.

Pearl

She introduces herself as a widow,
wearing her grief in long, somber dresses,
her hair disheveled, threaded with silver.

She keeps the windows closed year round,
air recycling endlessly. When she says,
he planted these azaleas, took this picture,

her voice cracks. Her body cannot hold
this much grief, it spills from her at the least
memory. No one's hand will again encircle

her wrist like a fine bracelet. She wants
no one to fix the watch from his father.
Slipping in and out of time signatures,

she drifts on hymns and ballads. She practices
calligraphy—it steadies her hand—
promises her daughters she'll visit, *soon.*

Neighbor

He sees me staking tomatoes.
Home ain't what it was.
He'd spoken to me before, after
I heard him cursing his wife.
It takes two to tangle, he growled then.

I rarely saw her. When she mowed
she didn't look up. Last spring her arm
was in a sling. Their sons rode bikes
round and round. The dogs dashed
the fence, barking madly. Doors slammed.

She took my boys, left the dogs.
Instant karma, I want to say, you
shouldn't've done what you did.
I used to be kinder, my heart opening
like a desert flower at the first drops of rain.

But I've listened to so many who refuse
to look deep into their own dark core,
afraid to discover what lurks there.
Nothing is ever their fault.
                       My neighbor

blames his wife's drinking, her folks,
this town. The sun beats down.
Mosquitoes whine.
Do I offer him a drink of water?
I brush the dirt from my hands.

Iryna

Before the pandemic forced our shops
to close, I often met Iryna for tea.
Even then she shrugged off any touch:
We don't do that way.

She would saunter in, unsmiling,
wearing a ragtag skirt and chiffon scarf,
hair loosening from a chignon,
trailing a scent of rose oil and musk.

As a child in Ukraine, she was left alone
to read and dream. *Nothing expected,
nothing to prove.* She wore her father's ring
on a chain around her neck.

An odd friendship—bookish, cool—
we loved Bergman and Jane Austen, preferred
cats to dogs, drank our tea black.
I was always on the verge of knowing her,

I thought. When I accused her once
of being here but not, she shrugged:
*All my life I am practicing
new ways to disappear.*

To Be True

For Bailey, age 15

In the months since your last visit,
your voice registers an octave lower,
your rangy bones have stretched another inch,
your hair has grown long and lustrous.
When you toss a lock back,
you are half prince, half colt.

You worry about people being shot in the street,
the ever-rising virus, your parents' marriage,
the future of this burning, flooding planet.
You wonder what you can do, who you
will become. To grow requires feeding—
fried chicken, mounds of ice cream.
To know yourself requires reading,
inventing, risking. And time,
a lifetime of questioning.

I wish I had answers. I want everything
I tell you to be true, as in level,
as in honest, though I myself
could use a dollop of faith.
None of the old stories work anymore.
Can you believe
we may be better than we seem?
I see simmering in you, and shimmering.
You look deep into the glass,
finish your milk in one long gulp.

Crows Above the Cemetery

Crows roost on the water-tower staves,
caw-scatting their dark chatter. Unruffled,
they miss nothing: me on my solitary walk,
that catbird dive-bombing a squirrel,
the grounds crew setting up to mow.

Tricksters, messengers, witches' familiars,
gossipers and spell casters, crows have been
onto us and part of us from the beginning,
wariness and brashness being taught in the nest.
Also thievery: take whatever shines and cache it.
Also clan behavior: call in the cousins to mob an interloper
or to mourn together, widows' feathers shining.

A few now land on the cemetery lawn,
swaggering like cops, giving me the side-eye
when I stop to watch: *Move along,
nothing to see here.* Before they lift
their tattered wings they laugh that laugh
that sounds like clicking bones.

I always see bluebirds

at the cemetery now,
always nod to anyone out walking.
What tenuous threads connect us,
afraid of another's touch or breathy laugh—
and just at a time, at my age, in this age,
when I'd like to be exuberant, to open
my throat and sing out like Pete Seeger did.

I'd like to ask him how we can go on
in such dark times.
Love, he would say, *love, always love.*
I would tell him how,
when my sister asked our mother
if she was ready to see Jesus,
she said *no!* so fast we had to laugh.

Pete might say the veil
between worlds is transparent,
we can pass through it
forwards and backwards anytime.
I'd ask him to sing and he would, with joy,
he'd make his favorite tarnished banjo
ring silver in the pearly light.

Census 2020

How many live in your heart?
How many are on fire?
How many flooded out?

Who changes the diapers?
Does anyone tiptoe around
the rage of another?

Is anyone in the household
reading Ginsburg, Sappho,
Crime and Punishment?

Does anyone dream in color?
Do you happen to know the answer
to 21 down in today's crossword?

Has your household received
an eviction notice yet?
Did anyone in your household

march for justice, for peace?
If yes, is anyone still marching?
List the number of guns in your household

by type and intention.
Name your favorite songwriter.
Name your favorite movie.

Who prays, and to whom,
how often, and for what?
There is no right or wrong answer.

Who among you is not complicit?
Is anyone enjoying the last
of the summer tomatoes?

Some People

Some people mow and blow their lawn
at first light. Some plant milkweed
for monarchs. Some keep a dog
tethered to a tree. They may
or may not smoke on their porch.
Some will tell you a group of towhees
is called a teapot, some that a cheetah
does zero to sixty faster than a Ferrari.
Some people think whatever they say
someone else wants to hear.
Some will never wear polka dots.
Some seek enlightenment, some revenge.
These may be the same people. While
you are meditating you may wish harm
to the fucker who sideswiped your car.
You can love that cicadas sound like
secrets told to everyone, but hate the heat
they thrive on. Some people chase their partner
crying into the street. Some people aspire
to sainthood. Some fly a flag you want
to bleach or shred. Some are bowed
by a mantle of sorrow. Some have too much
time, some are actively dying. They may
be the same people. Some eat handfuls
of sunlight. Some hear children's voices
and think *ghosts*. Some do not know
what a ballad is, or a prayer. Some
pretend they care about nothing
but walk to the park every day anyway.

Boat Cloud

Inspired by a collage by Marcos Guinoza

This is where
I want to be:
standing on a cloud,
its vapors swirling upward,
steering with a gondola oar,

like this old man
who must be wise,
for his beard and hair
are long and white,
tousled by a light wind.

Or maybe he is foolish—
having wished himself here
he discovers how futile his effort,
and his countenance shows
not concentration but fear.
Though he looks like Moses
perhaps he has seen
there is no path to heaven.

Still in this moment
I float, facing him.
The wind is kind
and on we sail.

It is time to stop waiting

for us all to be safe,
for morning to start,
the mourning to stop.

The collective unconscious
is unraveling
every-which-way in the wind,

the *i-n-g*'s of present-continuous verbs
streaming like kite tails.
This world of *I want*, and *I am left wanting*.

Today's walk is like yesterday's,
only now. Change happens,
with or without me, whether

I choose to name this shade of sky
or identify which species of sparrow
flits into the sycamore.

When my neighbor says
Happy fall, I do not say back,
We are all falling.

But not everyone's smile
is sad—that girl in red
with her new red scooter

is laughing as she learns
the joy of the glide,
what it takes to own the sidewalk.

A Measure of Happiness

It takes a lightness of spirit to appreciate
bluebirds on a high wire, their blushing throats bared,

magnolias in bloom, like candles set for a dinner party,
each solitary mockingbird singing for its own pleasure,

the girl running gazelle-like across the intersection
with such *ballon*, such joy,

clouds grazing the sky like sheep in a deep-blue pasture.
I'm walking the first morning of June.

The dire story I was telling myself has not happened,
may not happen. All that knitting and unknitting,

needles clicking in the dark hours, for nothing.
I'd forgotten the teachings I once knew.

The next person I see I will love without judgment,
like a good sister. I will, I swear I will.

Let my heart swing open

like French doors to a garden of blowsy flowers,
saloon doors where Kitty serves shots of rye,
a screen door with a farm wife waving you in,

or let my heart be a picture window
through which I see everyone I have ever loved,
my breath steaming the glass, come in,

we'll turn up the party lights,
show all the passersby we're dancing,
or better yet, let's all spill out into the street,

my heart a village music festival—
welcome teachers, firefighters, cashiers, nurses,
shysters and spinsters, salsa dancers and skateboarders,

cat lovers, detasselers, twirlers and high-steppers,
come in your scuffed shoes, rhinestones, flannels,
I'll be a mirror reflecting all y'all's kindness,

your clumsy moves and broken bits,
your sad patience and patient wildness,
your generosity, crankiness, haunted dreams—

I'll be the hostess sprinkling blessings like petals,
saying, *The universe is here and so are we—
champagne for everyone!*

First Daughter

It is right that you, her first-born,
        were witness to our mother's labor
as she left this troubled realm.

She always said she did not remember
        the details of your birth—the ether—
claimed she didn't know she'd named you

for a goddess. Yet how like Diana
        you are, who loves the woods,
a contrarian who depends on no man's

good word, seeks no god's blessing.
        So much about you she never understood,
you found hard to forgive her for.

A waning gibbous moon rose
        the night she passed, you said,
when energy slows, a time to reconnect.

Near the end she could not
        call your name. It was enough
that you sat beside her on the bed,

told her, *You have been a good mother,*
        let go now,
your work here is done.

        For Dhyana

When I call you saintly

you say *hardly*, shake your head.
But you don't have to be
pierced by arrows or burned alive

to deserve the name:
I mean your ministrations
to our mother, your shepherding

her to her final home,
in your eyes a blue promise
to take care of her,

your wild silver hair
an aura of beneficence,
I mean the light in you

that always made her brighten,
wave, call out,
That's my son.

    For Elm

It Takes a Heart Like Mary's These Days

An immaculate heart

not innocent
but swept clean

with room for all

a heart that grieves
        gleams

tough   luminous
mother of pearl

a heart with windows
stained   mirrored

whose light suffuses
        reflects

O heart of mercy
we are weary

cradle us

For Days I've Felt Myself Unraveling

The thin moon hides behind a smear of clouds.
Mini-nightmares keep waking me up.

At dusk crows flew in from all directions.
Such a ruckus they made, harassing an owl.

I imagined it stoic, unblinking on a sturdy branch,
but maybe it was terrified.

Much-needed rain spatters, percussive
on the tin roof. Grumble of thunder.

I should join a choir or drum circle.
Make of my body an instrument,

prayed someone—one voice lifted
to the troubling, never-ending skies.

My Mother's Funeral

Blackbirds skim the cornstalks
bowed down from last night's storm.

We came early to sweep up debris,
scrub lichens off the family stones.

On a hand-crocheted tablecloth
we arranged flowers, photographs,

her favorite porcelain angel.
The law allows only a graveside service

with no more than fifty gathered.
Cousins and elders arrive, wearing masks.

We are awkward, hesitant to touch.
Their eyes say, *I am here for her, for you.*

Sweating in church clothes
under the unkind sun,

I want to lose myself in the cornfield,
howl like a coyote alone.

Here sits my husband, here my two sons,
here my oldest grandson.

I try not to look at the sad mound
of black dirt. Words are spoken

I try to make sense of.
If I cry now I won't stop.

My chest is a thin shield
my heart pounds against.

We are at our best at a funeral, I think.
Suddenly we are all singing.

Dear Cemetery

Thank you for holding these souls
I have known since childhood,
for keeping their remains behind
the wrought-iron gate, tucked in
by cornfields along a narrow county road.

Thank you for letting me
remember the teacher who always tucked
a hankie in her bosom,
the boy with the talking crow,
the barber in his starched white jacket,

the lady who wore a mink coat to the grocer's,
great aunt Emma who made ballerinas
out of hollyhocks, my cousin
with the flat stone that reads only *Baby*,
the uncle who caned chairs and once

whistled on the radio,
my grandfather in the holey cardigan
fragrant with cigar smoke,
my grandmother whose only advice
was *just keep moving,*

my mother
who forgot her own self,
my father
who waited for everyone to leave
before he'd let go.

Thank you for reminding me
of what's left of their presence,
for allowing me to place here
these bright bouquets
now being battered by the wind.

III.

Bearing/Witness

for Joseph Bathanti

What is the ratio
of all we love to all we fear,

what we reap to what we plant,
what we see to what's below,

man's greed to earth's bounty,
what remains to what we've lost,

I mean destroyed,
all we mourn to all that was, is, or ever shall be?

We are tired
of being

told to be patient, resilient, to trust
the long arc bending.

How much looking must we do,
how much looking away,

to enjoy a walk in what remains
of this side of wilderness?

It's hard work to believe—
not in God or angels but in us,

we who take and have been taken from
over and again and then some.

Yet if we do not stare despair in its face
(I hear you say) how will we recognize

the silver sliver of moon
when it hangs suspended like a dream?

Shadows

After God made light from chaos and saw His own shadow,
He knew we would need sin, omens, a dark floor show.

How can anyone's childhood be innocent when clothes
draped on a bedpost create an evil scarecrow?

When the poet dreamed of *trees filled with terrifying nightingales*,
he awoke to a new war beyond his smoky window.

Isabel Archer's *movement and glance were a question.*
Did the answer lie in the sighs of encroaching willows?

Projecting our damages onto another, *we send out a crow*,
reminding us, Jung wrote, to look for our shadow.

Each generation creates a last judgment scenario.
Of our streetlight imaginations, poetry is the shadow.

Though named for the prophetess Deborah, what do I know?
That I am old, still waiting, afraid of my own shadow.

Doing Yoga and Swatting Flies to a Recording by Vladimir Horowitz

for Jeff Hardin

I read your poems until my heart says stop—
in your words my own despair and scant hope,
black butterflies landing on dead seedpods.

The world is too much with us, Wordsworth knew.
Even on this island in northern Canada
the news intrudes. This morning is gray clouds,

pines and cedars, a kerfuffle of crows,
persistent crickets. To add to the sadness,
it's the first day of fall. I put on a recording

of Horowitz to do yoga to. It starts with
the youthful joy of Mozart,
moves to Chopin's melancholy chords,

then to the passion of Schubert's Impromptu,
ending with Moszkowski's rousing
Etude in F major. All these exquisite notes

were composed in times of war, poverty, plague,
as when Horowitz played them in 1985,
as now, as I listen in 2021. How long

has humankind been so unkind, and why,
as your poems ask, when there's beauty
to behold and be beholden to,

are we such tribal, fearful creatures?
When I lie down in corpse pose, I am close
to tears. I miss my mother, gone a year

from the small world she loved. Flies buzz
at the window. *Die, fucker!* I say
with each swat. My compassion

is cirrus thin, continually shredding,
this long grief exhausting but never
spent, like bad pennies, like wishes.

Why write, you ask, will this fever ever break?
Horowitz said, *To find their meaning,
one must look behind the notes.*

On the Anniversary of My Mother's Death

If only she could know I carry her
lightly in me always, a kindly hum.
She even passed on to me her dread
of flies—*germy, crawly things.*

If a fly strafed her hair or landed
on a drop of water, she'd shudder,
then deftly flick the flyswatter,
and it's goodbye, Charlie.

She'd have noted the flies arrived
early this year, buzzing and razzing
with *purposeless circumference,*
harassing the best and worst of us.

Their second pair of wings gyroscopic
balancers, they land, despised pests,
on our countertops and flesh, rub their feet
together, then lap up the salt and fluids.

No matter. Each fly goes to its death
ignorant, unloved, its compound eyes
open, having seen every which way
except into the future.

After Yogi Berra and Robert Frost

If the world were perfect, it wouldn't be.
We made too many wrong mistakes.
We've cut, burned, poisoned, left a legacy
of marauding. Every day the earth quakes.

We made too many wrong mistakes.
But if I list the harm we've done, are doing now—
marauders still making the earth shake—
these lines would be only a weary plowing

of the harm we've done, are doing now.
I'd rather write to see what I didn't know I knew.
Lines that wearily plow old ground
surprise neither writer me nor reader you:

I'd rather *find out what I didn't know I knew.*
That's Frost. Yogi said, *You can observe a lot*
by watching. To surprise myself and you
I should try to transcribe a mockingbird's song.

Life goes on: that's Frost, weary. Yogi observed
life askew, off the cuff, as jester, wise guy, sage.
If I could transcribe a mockingbird's song
I'd leave something new, delightful on the page.

We need more jesters, wise guys, sages.
Though I can't rewrite the marauders' legacy,
I'd like to leave some delight on this page.
If the world were perfect, it wouldn't be.

After centuries of grief, the women in black

still bring cakes and casseroles to your home,
help arrange the ceremonial flowers,
hold the hands of the grieving in their own.

Because they are ancient and have borne
many deaths, they themselves are beyond
wails and tears, beyond tearing

their garments, bathing their heads with dust,
beyond having to tell children terrible stories

of wolves at the door and blood-stained floors,
where to find the nearest cupboard to hide in,

they are beyond their own bodies, they are
crows mobbing any intruder, crones
with mysterious spells, harpies crouching

on the lawns of those who refuse to see
how mourners must endure.

Behold their fierce claws and haggard faces.
See them spread wide their tattered wings
wild in the wind that made us.

Women Will Die

Who wouldn't rather drink
        coffee on the porch while
chickadees flit, chirping their names,

than read the headline *Women Will Die,*
        knowing the story that follows,
the ancient story:

women of the forbidden fruit,
        women hauling water at the well,
waiting to be chosen, women as bearers

of tidings, glad or otherwise,
        as bearers of the blame for what we did
with a man or a man did unto us,

forced to bear the fruit of that labor, *Women*
        Will Die, women as partners in the crime
of their bodies, of their daughters', their neighbors'

bodies, women as witnesses to centuries of
        mistakes were made,
women with secrets, *Help, I cannot bear this,*

women as strangers crossing state lines,
        as refugees, *Women Will Die,*
women of the underground, herbalists, healers,

women as villagers, warriors, sisters.
        Women too, alas, as enemies, the righteous
shouting in God's name, *So be it. Then, die.*

Eve, Again

> *"The world's old;/But the old world waits the hour to be renewed."*
> *Elizabeth Barrett Browning, Aurora Leigh*

Eve was the first namer, saying:
fragrant petal opener, flitterer of air,
silver swimmer, sharp-clawed pouncer.
She wandered through the perfect world
as everything beckoned,
everything responded.
At first her mate admired her grace,

her presence. No creator himself,
he knew not what to do.
They might have multiplied with ease,
but the Lord God wanted drama—
He tempted his characters,
rolled the dice, knowing odds are always
against those still awakening.

Banished to the desert, Eve took
her measure of shame and her mate's,
went deeply silent in her suffering.
Begat after begat in the stories named
only the fathers. What she knew was not
written but held in her body, then whispered
to her granddaughters, on down the line.

Of her words we've gleaned only glimpses,
warnings, shredded evidence. Despite
hangings and drownings, beatings and rapes,
despite being silenced, blamed, overruled,
women kept coming up for air and knowledge,
and we keep coming, wave after wave,
breathing steadily, spilling secrets, taking names.

Sing or Die

It's sixty degrees
in January. Janus reveals
his two faces.
              The sky,
a seamless blue but for two fat clouds,
streams past the past.
              Last night
when the Wolf Moon howled
I woke to troubled dreams.
              Now the sky
is not only sky, but omen,
a scrim Cassandra
looks through, knowing her predictions
must always go unheeded.

              I remind myself
to greet each moment as it arises.
              To notice is only
the first step. To speak is the second.
Then *to do*—but what?
              How lost
we humans act, or are.
              And yet
each morning I wake
mostly happy to be here,
to drink hot tea and watch
birds splash in the bath,
talk to someone I love.
              A mockingbird
lands on a bare branch,
tilts its head:
              sing or die.

Ritual

Supple, serious, this ring of women
sing-chant our questions toward the moon,
hopeful our devotion, our action—arms,
faces lifted, bodies swaying, voices
separate yet together as one—
are observed not by a judging god but
by a wild presence, the source of life, pure,
savage, whole. We chant not for paradise,
which failed Eve and her daughters forever,
but for earth restored. We chant in the name,
in the blood, of our grandmothers and in
our own blood, and our voices saturate
the steadfast trees, the windy lake, the tired
ground holding us up. Surely in this clearing,
where wildflowers and prairie grass still flourish,
we are heard, our song lyrical, damaged,
rising in and out of harmony. This
kinship, fleeting, holy, charges the air,
the earth we mourn and celebrate, our
fragile, passing selves. We witness this.
Dew on our feet. The moon in all her fullness.

Prayer

A bee lazes over
the wine glass rim.
The glass is chilled,
the wine crisp. This
early evening everything
is so delicate
I dare not move.
To be still, a gift,
to be here, another.
My heart, ragged
with wear and grief,
skips a half step
and begins to hum.
Let me hold this moment
before the sting.

What cannot be said will be wept

My mother, generous and kind,
sang hymns off-key around the house,
spoke of Jesus as if he lived next door.
No one who knew her doubted
she'd spend forever-after in heaven.

So why, two years after her death,
do I dream of her in a bleaker place?
She wears a white flannel nightgown
with faded pink rosebuds.
Her hair needs to be brushed.
I look out the rain-streaked window,
see our sadness reflected there.

I never thought I'd end up like this,
she says. I want to comfort her,
but my voice catches. The words
I want to say separate into letters
that fall like rain, and dissolve.

Memorial Day

The way waves of wind push the cloud
of starlings forward. The way
I no longer count Covid stats
or the days since my mother's passing.
The way we expect to be lied to. The way
we cannot stay present but for a moment,
and a moment passes into memory
or is forgotten, like our deepest dreams.
The alarm of clocks, the desire to turn back.
How can one bear to write
more children were slaughtered,
or write anything afterwards?
Crows own the bright blue playground.
The weight of each step:
one foot, another.
Shirtsleeves on the clothesline beckon.
Light trembles—

Today

I am done with dying for the day,

done with death, which has edged
my paper in black for too long,

which tumbles, bright and spinning,
from the shivering trees. Today

the sky is crisp, blue edged with clouds,
the sun shines on a dappled cat drowsing.

I bow to the town's oldest magnolia,
to the crickets' incessant chirping,

to the burnt-umber earth
ants are tunneling into.

Today I do not mourn what passes
or yearn for what is yet to be.

The crow gliding high knows
the present is a gift given and received,

the purpose of each step
is to take me to the next.

I asked if his compassion

was misspent on those
who'd done terrible things,

disguised themselves,
despised themselves,

who had fallen
into a well without footholds,

who believed they deserved
to shiver in the dark water,

each in his own well,
the only music they heard

was what they made paddling
and its hollow echo.

I knew he had a way—
a soft voice, a suffusing light—

of coaxing out the small animal
of those who did not

ever want to be seen.
He told me

so far he'd never run out of kindness,
it was a spring that,

after every giving,
kept refilling.

Canada Day

Crows chuff in the pine enclave.
I like to spy on them
knowing they know,

no window
between us, only saturated air,
no one else out yet.

A wasp drifts. There's a whisk
of insects in nettle, dock,
amaranth and spurge.

Birds-foot trefoil, bright
yellow in the sun,
begins to unshadow itself.

Stillness is never still.
Sadness is not all I hold.

I believe joy is quietly lurking,
waiting for this fountain pen's ink
to flow, for me to see words

as I set them down, to show
I appreciate what little I know.

End of Vacation

Monarchs fritter in the milkweed.
The cool air brushes my skin, my hair.
Nothing here cares who I think I am.

Home is neither here nor there.
Geese and cranes gather
before the long migration.

Days spool, spiders weave. I am old,
I guess, but do not know whether
I am becoming or unbecoming.

My mother's spirit appears
in the slightest light, in
that phraseless melody the wind does.

Victory comes late, Emily wrote,
but what is it to be victorious,
over whom or what?

When I read about a canyon
10,000 feet deep, I wonder if that
would be the way to go,

to leap, as in a dream I had,
and truly believe
this world is not conclusion—

or if not that, at least
to feel the rush of falling
not as terror but as bliss.

When You Invite in a Dream

You never know who will show up:
A teacher who makes you do impossible sums,
a judge who hides black wings under his gown,
your first love having his way with you.

It could be a beggar under haloed streetlights,
a queen in icy jewels doing crewelwork.
Maybe a wren, a talking crow,
a scrawny coyote, your long-lost cat.

There may appear a tarnished mirror, a too-red apple.
Your wedding ring slipping off your finger.
The sad glance of your father driving away.
A tidal wave sweeping your child out to sea.

When I asked for Durga astride her tiger
to unleash her divine wrath on the evil ones,
I got instead my young self stuck in a tree,
bees buzzing about, ominous clouds circling.

I'd like to dream of the old peasant again
planting seeds, the white mare beside him.
They always appear luminous in the moonlight.
He always assures me, *We still have time.*

A Wish for a New Year

Let's have a tempest in a teapot,
        some upstarts and whippersnappers,
                a lawn full of children
laughing with their whole bodies,

a teenage skateboarder with dreamy eyes
        zigzagging with grace,
                a somersaulting Jack Russell,
a magician releasing doves from his sleeves,

cafeteria ladies handing out
        Dixie cups of ice cream,
                a chime of wrens, a charm of finches,
a majorette spinning her glittering baton,

let's have a drum line, cymbals, piccolos,
        clarinets, brassy brass, smart stepping,
                with fireworks to come,
we need the good sass and frazzle,

a bountiful blue sky, anything
        to walk us catawampus across the talk
                of gripery, liars, and pettiness,
shooting deaths the highest on record,

I mean simple acts of kindness
        when we gather in the streets,
                everyday magic, the kind of mayhem
where no one gets hurt and all is forgiven.

Campfire

for Barrie, Manitoulin Island, September 11, 2022

All summer we swam in the cold, clean lake,
canoed, hiked, biked the farm roads,
watched sandhill cranes gather in hay fields,

heard jays and ravens trade their trash talk,
chickadees trilling through it all. Tonight
the wolf family calls from the woods:

a parent's howl, the pups yapping back.
We sit around the fire, our last this season.
Our hands smell of cedar, smoke, peaty scotch.

The wind shifts, the fire resettles.
Jupiter appears, then Saturn.
A saw-whet owl hoots its tugboat toot.

*Can we take this abundance home, be different
somehow?* you ask. Since I don't know I say nothing:
there are already too many words in the world.

Creatures among creatures, we only want
what's simple—food, water, quiet, sky.
Love. Safe distances. A planet breathing.

To the wren with the loud song

who wakes me each morning,
I am sorry, sorry, so so sorry,
for what you don't know is coming:
the maples on the patch of land
you fly from, whose orange-gold leaves
are now scattering in the wind, will be
dismembered this spring.

So too the other elders,
those who harbor the flutter of sparrows,
the red-bellied woodpecker,
cardinals, mockingbirds, jays,
from whose branches squirrels leap,
in whose shade mice and rabbits hide
from coyote, the trickster's shadow,

and the shrubs, scrub grass, volunteer saplings:
all will be gone by nesting time,
the ground churned up, scraped and leveled,
asphalted over. In their stead a clutch
of beige four-story apartments.

What we still have we offer to you.
The hundred-year-old pecan trees in our back yard
have room, the dogwoods, holly,
bay laurel, crape myrtles, and our neighbors'
azaleas, junipers, tulip tree.
We're putting up more birdbaths and feeders,
planting new trees.

Starting with the first shovelful of dirt,
I'll dedicate this work to you
and to those who will come after we're gone.

Notes

Most of these poems were written during the Covid pandemic, either on my daily walks in Mebane, North Carolina, or while vacationing in Manitoulin Island, Ontario, but have their roots in the Midwest.

"It Takes a Heart Like Mary's These Days": The title is from a line in the Joni Mitchell song "Don't Interrupt the Sorrow."
"Shadows": The phrase "trees filled with terrifying nightingales" is from *World Within World: The Autobiography of Stephen Spender*; "movement and glance were a question" is from *The Portrait of a Lady* by Henry James; "we send out a crow" is from *A Little Book on the Human Shadow* by Robert Bly; "Of our streetlight imaginations, poetry is the shadow" is a rewording of a line from Lawrence Ferlinghetti.
"On the Anniversary of My Mother's Death": the phrase "purposeless circumference" is from by Emily Dickinson's poem "From cocoon forth a butterfly."
"Women Will Die" was written just after the overturning of *Roe v. Wade*.
"Ritual" is a response to §VI of "Sunday Morning" by Wallace Stevens.
"What cannot be said will be wept": The title is a quote attributed to Sappho.
"Memorial Day": The last line is from a letter Emily Dickinson wrote to her sister-in-law Susan after the death of Susan's young son Gib.
"End of Vacation": Phrases in italics are from Emily Dickinson poems.

Acknowledgments

I am grateful to editors of these journals and anthologies for publishing the following poems, sometimes in a different form or with a different title:

Cordella: "First Daughter"
Flush Left: A River Sings (Indolent Books 2023): "You've lived many lifetimes like this"
Indelible: "To Be True," "It Takes a Heart Like Mary's These Days"
North Carolina Literary Review: "When I call you saintly," "Heading West," "Daguerrologue" (all finalists in James Applewhite contests)
Persimmon Tree: "Campfire," "Sing or Die"
Pine Straw: "Chime," "After Church"
Poetry South: "Forgotten," "After centuries of grief, the women in black"
Quartet Journal: "Iryna"
Red Fez: "Crows in the Cemetery"
Relief: A Journal of Art and Faith: "Shadows," "When You Invite in a Dream"
Silver Birch Press: "Falling and Falling Apart," "Let my heart swing open like French doors," "Someone called my name on the stairs"
Tar River Poetry: "Census 2020," "Bearing/Witness." "Ritual"
The Healing Muse: "School Picture, Second Grade," "What cannot be said will be wept"
The Phare: "The Babysitter," "Memorial Day"
The Power of the Feminine I (Thresh Press): "The Annunciation"
Triggerfish Literary Review: "Wild Horses," "I always see bluebirds," "Half Wolf," "Holy Hell," "Some People," "Doing Yoga and Swatting Flies to a Recording by Vladimir Horowitz"
Verse-Virtual: "To the wren with the loud song"

Endless love for Barrie, Bryce, Darcy, Bailey, and Bennett, without whom I have no idea who I might be; for my sibs, Dhyana, Elmer, and Eric, our parents and extended family; and to my Midwest childhood and adolescent friends: You all have inspired me. Thank you to the Black Socks Poets and Deborah Pope, who read and commented on early versions of these poems, to the North Carolina writing and theater communities, and to my neighbors for their presence. I deeply appreciate the caregivers at Arbor Terrace in Naperville, Illinois, especially during the Covid lock-down; they held the phone or laptop for my mother whenever I called. For my friends of spirit: no words will suffice. Thank you to Patricia Thompson and Robert Canipe at Redhawk Publications for publishing my manuscript with care.

About the author

Poet and playwright Debra Kaufman is the author of *God Shattered, Delicate Thefts, The Next Moment* (all from Jacar Press), and *A Certain Light* (Emrys Press), as well as three chapbooks. A Midwest native, she lives in central North Carolina.

http://www.Debrakaufman.info

www.ingramcontent.com/pod-product-compliance
Lightning Source LLC
Chambersburg PA
CBHW021021090426
42738CB00007B/851